# Classic Recipes of
# WALES

## TRADITIONAL FOOD AND COOKING
## IN 25 AUTHENTIC DISHES

ANNETTE YATES

LORENZ BOOKS

This edition is published by Lorenz Books,
an imprint of Anness Publishing Ltd, 108 Great Russell Street,
London WC1B 3NA; info@anness.com

www.lorenzbooks.com; www.annesspublishing.com;
twitter: @Anness_Books

If you like the images in this book and would like to investigate
using them for publishing, promotions or advertising, please visit
our website www.practicalpictures.com for more information.

A CIP catalogue record for this book is available from
the British Library.

Publisher: Joanna Lorenz
Project Editor: Kate Eddison
Photographer: Craig Robertson
Food Stylist: Fergal Connolly
Prop Stylist: Helen Trent
Designer: Nigel Partridge
Production Controller: Rosie Anness

NOTES

Bracketed terms are intended for American readers. For all recipes,
quantities are given in both metric and imperial measures and, where
appropriate, in standard cups and spoons. Follow one set of measures,
but not a mixture, because they are not interchangeable.
Standard spoon and cup measures are level.
1 tsp = 5ml, 1 tbsp = 15ml, 1 cup = 250ml/8fl oz.
Australian standard tablespoons are 20ml. Australian readers should
use 3 tsp in place of 1 tbsp for measuring small quantities.
American pints are 16fl oz/2 cups. American readers should use
20fl oz/2.5 cups in place of 1 pint when measuring liquids.
Electric oven temperatures in this book are for conventional ovens.
When using a fan oven, the temperature will probably need to be
reduced by about 10–20°C/20–40°F. Since ovens vary, you should
check with your manufacturer's instruction book for guidance.
The nutritional analysis given for each recipe is calculated per portion
(i.e. serving or item), unless otherwise stated. If the recipe gives a
range, such as Serves 4–6, then the nutritional analysis will be for the
smaller portion size, i.e. 6 servings. The analysis does not include
optional ingredients, such as salt added to taste.
Medium (US large) eggs are used unless otherwise stated.

PUBLISHER'S NOTE

# contents

# introduction

Wales has a strong tradition of living off the land that stretches back as far as the ancient Celts and has survived into the 21st century in some areas. Traditionally, the fare is simple but wholesome, designed to satisfy the hearty appetites of hard-working farmers, coal miners, quarry workers and fishermen.

Surprisingly little is documented about the early cooking of Wales. Generally, traditional culinary skills were passed on from mothers to their daughters as they worked together in the kitchen, rather than being written down. In fact, so little had been recorded that the culinary heritage of Wales was in danger of being lost completely after women began working in jobs outside the home. That is, until Minwel Tibbott, a staff member at the Welsh Folk Museum, began voice-recording the memories of old people during the late 20th century.

Today, Wales has embraced its culinary heritage and is now justifiably proud of its food culture. It enjoys world recognition for much of its produce and its chefs are regarded as among the best in the world.

Wales is a mountainous land with deep river valleys. It has outstanding areas of natural beauty, from craggy peaks and peaceful valleys to tranquil reservoirs and picturesque lakes. With around 80 per cent of the land dedicated to agriculture, the varied and contrasting landscape influences the food of the region.

*Above: The Brecon Beacons is famed for its breathtaking landscape.*
*Left: The scenic river Wye meanders through rich, agricultural lowlands.*

The rural uplands were once dominated by goats and cattle, but the booming wool trade saw vast numbers of sheep being reared too.

In common with most hilly regions in Britain, oats and barley have long been staple crops in the rural uplands, where the climate is wet and cold. The lowlands, with their fertile valleys and rivers, provide perfect conditions for wheat and vegetable crops, and an environment where dairy herds thrive. The coastline of Wales has been a rich source of fish and other seafood,

and the coastal marshlands are home to a popular speciality of the region, saltmarsh lamb.

Other native ingredients that remain central to Welsh cooking include fresh leeks and cabbages; fruits like apples, damsons and plums; dairy products such as milk, butter, cream and cheese; salmon and brown trout from the fast-flowing rivers; herring, mackerel, cockles, mussels and scallops from the ocean; traditional laverbread (a seaweed boiled to make a soft, dark green mass); tender cuts

*Above left: The peninsula of Wales is surrounded by the sea on three sides.*
*Top: Sheep perch precariously on steep mountains above deep valleys.*
*Above right: Herds of cattle roam on farmland in West Glamorgan.*

of mountain lamb; beef from age-old breeds of Welsh cattle; time-honoured faggots and delicious cured bacon.

These classic ingredients are used to produce an array of delectable dishes, the best of which are included in this book.

# appetizers, light meals and breakfasts

Anyone visiting a Welsh household is likely to be offered traditional favourites and light bites. This may be a steaming bowl of cawl (a hearty soup) made with leeks and potatoes and flavoured with home-cured bacon, or a savoury dish in which cheese, eggs or leeks star as the main ingredients. To begin the day, the classic full breakfast is usually accompanied by the Welsh delicacy laverbread, served on the side or mixed with oatmeal and cooked in hot bacon fat.

*Left: Potatoes, leeks and cabbage have long been staples in the Welsh kitchen and are incorporated in a wide range of traditional dishes.*

# leek soup

This is an adaptation of a traditional cooking method, where bacon, vegetables and water were left to simmer in the pot all day. It often made two courses or meals – the bacon and vegetables for one and the cawl or broth for the other.

**3** Meanwhile, finely chop the parsley and set aside.

**4** Remove the bacon. Either slice it and serve separately or cut it into chunks and return to the pan.

**5** Season, then bring to the boil again. Add the dark green leeks and parsley, simmer for 5 minutes, then serve.

### Serves 4–6

1 unsmoked bacon joint, such as
    corner or collar, weighing about
    1kg/2¼lb, trimmed of excess fat
1 large carrot, peeled
1 large main-crop potato, peeled
500g/1¼lb/4½ cups leeks,
    thoroughly washed and
    finely sliced
15ml/1 tbsp fine or medium oatmeal
handful of fresh parsley
salt and ground black pepper

**1** Put the bacon into a large pan and pour over enough cold water to cover. Bring to the boil, then discard the water. Add 1.5 litres/2½ pints fresh cold water, bring to the boil again, and simmer, covered, for 30 minutes.

**2** Finely chop the carrot and slice the potato. Add to the pan with the white and pale green parts of the leeks and the oatmeal. Bring to the boil, cover and simmer gently for 30-40 minutes.

Per portion Energy 273kcal/1135kJ; Protein 18.8g; Carbohydrate 10.9g, of which sugars 3.5g; Fat 17.3g, of which saturates 6.3g; Cholesterol 53mg; Calcium 33mg; Fibre 2.7g; Sodium 1550mg

# Welsh rarebit

In its simplest form, Welsh Rarebit, *Caws wedi pobi*, would traditionally have consisted
of a chunk of bread and a large slice of hard cheese, each toasted in front of the fire.
Before the cheese had softened too much, it was served on top of the crisp bread.

**Serves 2**

2 thick slices of bread
soft butter, for spreading
10ml/2 tsp ready-made mustard
   of your choice
100g/3¾oz Cheddar-style cheese,
   such as Llanboidy, or crumbly
   cheese such as Caerphilly, sliced
ground black pepper
pinch of paprika or cayenne pepper

**1** Put the bread on the rack of a grill
(broiler) pan and place under a hot
grill until both sides are lightly toasted.

**2** Spread one side of each slice of
toast with butter and then a little
mustard (or to taste). Top with cheese.

**3** Put under the grill until the cheese
is soft, bubbling and golden brown.

**4** Sprinkle with a little black pepper
and paprika or cayenne and serve
immediately.

**Variation**

As an alternative method, use
a mixture of cheeses, grated and
stirred together with the butter
and mustard before spreading them
on the toast and grilling (broiling).

Per portion Energy 386kcal/1611kJ; Protein 18.4g; Carbohydrate 25.8g, of which sugars 1.4g; Fat 23.7g, of which saturates 13.5g; Cholesterol 59mg; Calcium 442mg; Fibre 0.8g; Sodium 652mg

# Anglesey eggs

This delicious dish of potatoes, leeks, eggs and cheese sauce, *Wyau Ynys Môn*, is traditional to the Isle of Anglesey. Instead of browning the dish in the oven, you may prefer to finish it off under a medium-hot grill.

### Serves 4

500g/1¼lb potatoes, peeled
3 leeks, sliced
6 eggs, hard-boiled and cooled
50g/2oz/3 tbsp butter
600ml/1 pint/2½ cups milk
50g/2oz/½ cup plain (all-purpose) flour
100g/3¾oz/1 cup Caerphilly
  cheese, grated
salt and ground black pepper

**1** Cook the potatoes in boiling, lightly salted water for 15 minutes. Cook the leeks in a little water for 10 minutes.

**2** Preheat the oven to 200°C/400°F/ Gas 6. Drain and mash the potatoes. Drain the leeks. Stir them into the potatoes with black pepper to taste. Remove the shells from the eggs and cut in half or into quarters lengthways.

**3** Cut the butter into small pieces, then put in a pan with the milk and flour. Bring to the boil, stirring. Bubble gently for 2 minutes, until thickened. Off the heat, stir in half the cheese and season.

**4** Put the eggs in ovenproof dishes and surround with potato. Top with cheese sauce and the remaining cheese. Cook in the hot oven for 15–20 minutes.

Per portion Energy 540kcal/2259kJ; Protein 26.6g; Carbohydrate 41.3g, of which sugars 12.3g; Fat 30.6g, of which saturates 16.2g; Cholesterol 345mg; Calcium 471mg; Fibre 5g; Sodium 443mg

# cheese pudding

Old recipes for this classic dish, *Pwdin caws wedi bobi*, involved cooking layers
of toasted bread and cheese in the custard mixture. Serve it with green vegetables,
such as beans or broccoli, if you like, or with a crisp salad.

**Serves 4**

225g/8oz/2 cups grated mature
   Cheddar-style cheese
115g/4oz/2 cups fresh breadcrumbs
600ml/1 pint/2½ cups milk
40g/1½oz/3 tbsp butter
3 eggs, beaten
5ml/1 tsp mustard of your choice
   or 2.5ml/½ tsp mustard powder
salt and ground black pepper

**1** Preheat the oven to 200°C/400°F/
Gas 6. Butter the insides of a 1.2 litre/
2 pint/5 cups ovenproof soufflé dish.

**2** Mix three-quarters of the cheese with
the breadcrumbs. Set aside. Put the
remaining ingredients into a pan and
stir well. Heat gently, stirring, until the
butter has just melted (if the mixture
gets too hot, the eggs will start to set).

**3** Stir the warm liquid into the cheese
mixture and tip into the prepared
dish. Scatter the remaining cheese
evenly over the top.

**4** Put the pudding into the hot oven
and cook for about 30 minutes
or until golden brown and just set
(a knife inserted into the centre
should come out clean).

Per portion Energy 449Kcal/1859kJ; Protein 31.8g; Carbohydrate 0g, of which sugars 0g; Fat 35.7g, of which saturates 8.3g; Cholesterol 123mg; Calcium 96mg; Fibre 0g; Sodium 1.5g

# leek and goat's cheese tart

Wonderful goat's cheeses are made in Wales today, from soft cheese and soft-rind logs to hard varieties that are ideal for cooking. For strong cheeses, you may want to use the smaller quantity listed. This tart is best served hot or at room temperature.

### Serves 6

75g/3oz/¾ cup hazelnuts, skinned
175g/6oz/1½ cups plain
   (all-purpose) flour
115g/4oz/½ cup butter, chilled
   and cut into small cubes
15ml/1 tbsp olive oil
350g/12oz/3 cups leeks, thinly sliced
5 eggs, lightly beaten
450ml/¾ pint single (light) cream
2.5ml/½ tsp wholegrain mustard
175–225g/6–8oz/1½–2 cups grated
   hard goat's cheese, such as Merlin
salt and ground black pepper

### Variation

This is also good with crumbled Caerphilly cheese: use the larger quantity listed in the ingredients.

**1** Toast the hazelnuts in a dry frying pan, in a hot oven or under the grill (broiler), until golden. Leave to cool, roughly chop half and finely chop the rest.

**2** Sift the flour and seasoning into a large bowl and stir in the finely chopped nuts. Using your fingertips, rub in the butter. Sprinkle over about 45ml/3 tbsp cold water, mix until it begins to stick together, then gather it into a ball. Roll out the pastry and line a 25cm/10in flan tin (pan). Put in the refrigerator for 10–25 minutes to rest.

**3** Put a baking sheet in the oven and preheat to 200°C/400°F/Gas 6. Put the oil and leeks into a pan and cook until soft, stirring occasionally. (Alternatively, place in a covered microwave-proof dish and microwave on full power for 5 minutes.)

**4** Prick the base of the pastry case and line with baking parchment and dried beans. Cook on the baking sheet for 10 minutes. Remove the paper and beans and brush the pastry with egg. Return to the oven for 3–4 minutes.

**5** Mix the remaining eggs with the cream, mustard, half the cheese and a little seasoning. Stir the mixture into the leeks and pour into the pastry case. Sprinkle the remaining cheese and hazelnuts on top. Cook in the oven for 30 minutes.

Per portion Energy 683kcal/2835kJ; Protein 20.7g; Carbohydrate 26.9g, of which sugars 4g; Fat 55g, of which saturates 27.3g; Cholesterol 267mg; Calcium 381mg; Fibre 3.1g; Sodium 409mg

# Glamorgan sausages

When is a sausage not a sausage? When it is a Glamorgan sausage! These famous meat-free concoctions were made at least as far back as the 1850s.

**3** Lightly whisk the reserved egg white. Coat each sausage in flour, then the whisked egg white and finally, fresh breadcrumbs.

**4** Heat some oil in a deep-fat fryer or large pan to 180°C/350°F. Lower the sausages into the oil and cook for 5 minutes until they are crisp and golden brown. Lift out, drain on kitchen paper and serve immediately.

**Makes 8**

150g/5½oz/3 cups fresh breadcrumbs, plus extra for coating
100g/3¾oz/1 cup mature (sharp) Caerphilly cheese, grated
1 small leek, thinly sliced
15–30ml/1–2 tbsp chopped fresh herbs, such as parsley and thyme
5ml/1 tsp mustard powder
2 eggs
milk, to mix
plain (all-purpose) flour, for coating
vegetable oil, for deep-frying
salt and ground black pepper

**1** In a large mixing bowl, stir together the breadcrumbs, cheese, leek, herbs, mustard and seasoning. Separate one egg and lightly beat the yolk with the whole egg (reserving the white). Stir the beaten eggs into the breadcrumb mixture. Add sufficient milk to gather the mixture into a sticky (not wet) ball.

**2** Using your hands, divide the mixture into eight and shape into sausages of equal size. Cover and chill in the refrigerator for about 1 hour, or until needed.

Per portion Energy 202kcal/844kJ; Protein 7.6g; Carbohydrate 17.6g, of which sugars 1g; Fat 11.5g, of which saturates 3.8g; Cholesterol 60mg; Calcium 134mg; Fibre 1g; Sodium 251mg

# laverbread cakes and bacon

Laverbread forms an integral part of the full Welsh breakfast. Here, it is combined with oatmeal and shaped into small cakes. It tastes best when cooked in bacon fat.

**Serves 4**

200g/7oz laverbread
10ml/2 tsp fresh lemon juice
65g/2½oz/½ cup fine oatmeal
10ml/2 tsp oil
8 bacon rashers (strips)
salt and ground black pepper

**1** Mix the laverbread, lemon juice and oatmeal. Season with salt and black pepper and leave for 5 minutes.

**2** Heat the oil in a pan, add the bacon and cook over medium-high heat until golden brown. Lift out and keep warm.

**3** Drop spoonfuls of the laverbread mixture into the hot pan, flattening them gently with the back of the spoon. Cook over medium heat for a minute or two on each side until crisp and golden brown.

**4** Serve the hot laverbread cakes with the bacon rashers.

**Variation**

Add about 100g/3¾oz shelled cooked cockles (small clams) to the laverbread and oatmeal mixture in step 1. You could also add a little finely grated lemon rind, together with the lemon juice in step 1, if you like

Per portion Energy 286kcal/1204kJ; Protein 14.1g; Carbohydrate 33.8g, of which sugars 1.4g; Fat 11.7g, of which saturates 3.1g; Cholesterol 23mg; Calcium 65mg; Fibre 3.7g; Sodium 923mg

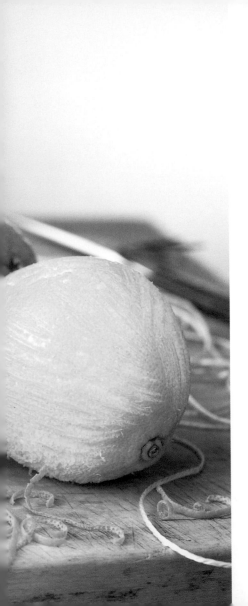

# main courses

Wales enjoys a wonderful variety of fish from its extensive coastline, lakes and fast-flowing rivers. From the sea comes herring, mackerel, cockles and scallops, and running the rivers are wild brown trout and salmon. The Welsh diet has always relied on plentiful supplies of meat too, since the days when most families fattened up a pig in the garden and cured their own bacon. Today, Welsh lamb and beef enjoy international recognition for their succulence and flavour, including the traditional saltmarsh lamb, which has revived in popularity.

*Left: Slowly roasted Saltmarsh lamb makes a wonderful meal for a special occasion.*

# baked salmon with herb-and-lemon mayonnaise

Years ago, it was usual to poach a whole salmon in milk. Today, it is more likely to be cooked in the oven. Leave the head on or take it off, as you prefer.

## Serves 6

1.3kg/3lb fresh whole salmon
  or sewin (sea trout), cleaned
1 small lemon, thinly sliced
handful of parsley sprigs
salt and ground black pepper
butter or oil, for greasing

### For the mayonnaise

300ml/½ pint/1¼ cups mayonnaise
30ml/2 tbsp natural (plain) yogurt
  or single (light) cream
finely grated rind of ½ lemon
30ml/2 tbsp finely chopped
  fresh chives
15ml/1 tbsp finely chopped
  fresh parsley
squeeze of lemon juice (optional)

**1** Start by preheating the oven to 180°C/350°F/Gas 4. Rinse the cleaned salmon or sewin, both inside and out, under cold running water, and then pat it dry with kitchen paper. Season the cavity with a little salt and pepper and spread half the lemon slices and the parsley sprigs inside the fish.

**2** Grease a large sheet of thick foil and lay the fish on it. Put the remaining lemon slices and parsley on top. Fold the foil over to make a loose, but secure, parcel. Put in the hot oven and bake for 40 minutes.

**3** Stir together the mayonnaise ingredients, adding lemon juice to taste.

**4** Remove the fish from the oven and tear open the foil. Peel away the skin, cutting around the head and tail with a sharp knife and discarding the parsley and lemon from the top of the fish. Carefully turn the fish over and repeat with the other side.

**5** Lift the salmon on to a warmed serving plate and serve with the herb-and-lemon mayonnaise.

Per portion Energy 551kcal/2289kJ; Protein 35.9g; Carbohydrate 1.5g, of which sugars 1.2g; Fat 44.7g, of which saturates 7.3g; Cholesterol 182mg; Calcium 84mg; Fibre 0.4g; Sodium 362mg

# scallops with bacon and sage

Scallops are fished off the west coast and, in particular, off Anglesey. Here, their sweetness is complemented by the addition of bacon. This dish is great served with marsh samphire, an edible coastal plant, when it is in season.

## Serves 2

4 streaky (fatty) bacon
    rashers (strips)
15ml/1 tbsp olive oil
2–3 fresh sage leaves, chopped
small piece of butter
8 large or 16 small scallops
15ml/1 tbsp fresh lemon juice
100ml/3½fl oz dry cider or
    white wine

1 Cut the bacon into 2.5cm/1in strips. Heat a frying pan and add the oil, bacon and sage. Cook over a medium heat, stirring often, until the bacon is golden. Lift out and keep warm.

2 Add the butter to the pan and when hot add the scallops. Cook for about 1 minute on each side until browned. Lift out and keep warm with the bacon.

3 Add the lemon juice and dry cider or white wine to the pan and, scraping up any sediment, bring the mixture just to the boil. Continue bubbling gently until the mixture has reduced to just a few tablespoons of syrupy sauce.

4 Serve the scallops and bacon with the sauce drizzled over.

Per portion Energy 179kcal/745kJ; Protein 15.6g; Carbohydrate 1.9g, of which sugars 0.2g; Fat 10.4g, of which saturates 3.3g; Cholesterol 42mg; Calcium 19mg; Fibre 0g; Sodium 414mg

# trout with bacon

Wrapping trout this way helps to retain moisture and adds flavour. If you are lucky enough to obtain wild trout, you will appreciate how its earthy flavour works with the bacon and leek. Make sure you use dry-cure bacon for this traditional *Brithyll a bacwn*.

## Serves 4

4 trout, each weighing about
  225g/8oz, cleaned
a handful of parsley sprigs
4 lemon slices, plus lemon
  wedges to serve
8 large leek leaves
8 streaky (fatty) bacon rashers
  (strips), rinds removed
salt and ground black pepper

**1** Preheat the oven to 180°C/350°F/ Gas 4. Rinse the trout, inside and out, under cold running water, then pat dry with kitchen paper. Season the cavities and put a few parsley sprigs and a slice of lemon into each.

**2** Wrap two leek leaves, then two bacon rashers, spiral fashion around each fish. Secure the ends with wooden cocktail sticks (toothpicks).

**3** Lay the fish in a shallow ovenproof dish, side by side, head next to tail.

**4** Bake for about 20 minutes, until the bacon is brown and the leeks are tender. The trout should be cooked through; check by inserting a sharp knife into the thickest part.

**5** Chop the remaining parsley, then sprinkle over the trout and serve.

Per portion Energy 324kcal/1357kJ; Protein 44.4g; Carbohydrate 0.4g, of which sugars 0.3g; Fat 16.1g, of which saturates 5.1g; Cholesterol 174mg; Calcium 60mg; Fibre 0.3g; Sodium 997mg

# mackerel with onions

When buying mackerel, look for really fresh fish with bright eyes and bluish-green tinges on the skin. In this recipe, *Mecryll gyda winwns*, the sweetness of the onions and the sharpness of the vinegar complement the oily flesh of the mackerel.

**4** Remove the lid, increase the heat and continue cooking until the onions are golden brown.

**5** Add the apple juice and vinegar. Boil until the mixture is well reduced, thick and syrupy. Remove from the heat, stir in the herbs and season to taste. Remove the bay leaf. Serve the onions with the mackerel.

### Serves 2

1 garlic clove
2 mackerel, cleaned
15ml/1 tbsp oil
1 large onion, very thinly sliced
1 bay leaf
150ml/¼ pint/⅔ cup apple juice
   or cider
30ml/2 tbsp wine vinegar
15ml/1 tbsp finely chopped fresh
   parsley or coriander (cilantro)
salt and ground black pepper

**1** Finely chop or crush the garlic. Make two or three shallow slashes down each side of each mackerel.

**2** Heat the oil in a frying pan, add the mackerel and cook over medium heat for 5–8 minutes on each side until just cooked. Lift out and keep warm.

**3** Add the onion, garlic and bay leaf to the pan, cover and cook gently for 10–15 minutes, stirring occasionally.

Per portion Energy 451kcal/1876kJ; Protein 30.5g; Carbohydrate 15.9g, of which sugars 13.5g; Fat 29.9g, of which saturates 5.6g; Cholesterol 80mg; Calcium 87mg; Fibre 2.4g; Sodium 98mg

# herrings with mustard

The west coast of Wales was famous for its herring catches. Fillets would be spread with mustard, rolled and cooked with potato, onion and apple, which was the inspiration for this dish, *Penwaig gyda mwstard*.

**Serves 2**

4–6 herrings, filleted
20–30ml/4–6 tsp
   wholegrain mustard
4–6 small young sage leaves
1 eating apple, quartered,
   cored and cut into
   thin wedges
wholemeal (whole-wheat)
   bread, to serve

**1** Preheat the oven to 180°C/350°F/ Gas 4. Rinse the herrings under cold running water and dry them inside and out with kitchen paper.

**2** Open the fish and lay them, skin side down, on a board or a clean work surface. Spread each herring with 5ml/1 tsp wholegrain mustard and tear one sage leaf over each.

**3** Lay the apple wedges lengthways along one side of each fish, overlapping them. Fold the other half over.

**4** Oil a baking tray (or line it with baking parchment) and lift the herrings on to it.

**5** Cook for 20 minutes, until cooked through and beginning to brown at the edges. Serve with wholemeal bread.

Per portion Energy 209kcal/870kJ; Protein 18.5g; Carbohydrate 3.5g, of which sugars 3.5g; Fat 13.5g, of which saturates 3.3g; Cholesterol 50mg; Calcium 102mg; Fibre 1.6g; Sodium 128mg

# fish pie

*Pastai bysgod* is a traditional fish pie, using a combination of white fish and smoked haddock, with a distinct Welsh flavour. You can replace the puff pastry topping with mashed potato, if you prefer. Laverbread adds an extra twist of Welsh character.

**Serves 4**

225g/8oz skinless white fish,
  such as hake, haddock or cod
225g/8oz skinless smoked
  haddock or cod
450ml/¾ pint/scant 2 cups milk
25g/1oz/2 tbsp butter
25g/1oz/¼ cup plain
  (all-purpose) flour
good pinch of freshly
  grated nutmeg
1 leek, thinly sliced
200g/7oz shelled cooked cockles
  (small clams)
30ml/2 tbsp laverbread (optional)
30ml/2 tbsp finely chopped
  fresh parsley
1 sheet ready-rolled puff pastry
salt and ground black pepper

**1** Preheat the oven to 200°C/400°F/Gas 6. Put the white and smoked fish in a pan with the milk. Heat until the milk barely comes to the boil, then cover and poach gently for about 8 minutes or until the fish is just cooked. Lift the fish out, reserving the liquid. Break into flakes, discarding any bones.

**2** Melt the butter, stir in the flour and cook for 1–2 minutes. Remove and stir in the reserved cooking liquid. Stir over medium heat until the sauce thickens.

**3** Stir in the fish flakes and their juices. Add the nutmeg and season to taste. Add the leek, cockles, laverbread and parsley to the sauce and spoon into a 1.2 litre/2 pint/5 cup ovenproof dish.

**4** Brush the edges of the dish with water. Unroll the pastry and lay it over the top of the dish, trimming it to fit.

**5** Use the pastry off-cuts to make decorative fish or leaves for the top, brushing each one with a little water to help them stick.

**6** Cook in the oven for 30 minutes, until the pastry is puffed and golden brown.

Per portion Energy 573kcal/2401kJ; Protein 36.8g; Carbohydrate 41g, of which sugars 7.3g; Fat 31.2g, of which saturates 4.7g; Cholesterol 92mg; Calcium 270mg; Fibre 1.2g; Sodium 1084mg

# roast chicken with leek, laver and lemon stuffing

The three 'Ls' – leek, laver and lemon – complement each other beautifully to make a light stuffing that marries perfectly with the taste and texture of roast chicken.

## Serves 4–6

1.4–1.8kg/3–4lb oven-ready chicken
1 small onion, quartered
½ lemon, roughly chopped
2 garlic cloves, halved
olive oil or melted butter

### For the stuffing

30ml/2 tbsp olive oil
2 rindless bacon rashers (strips), finely chopped
1 small leek, thinly sliced
1 garlic clove, crushed or finely chopped
30ml/2 tbsp laverbread
150g/5oz/1¼ cups fresh breadcrumbs
finely grated rind and juice of ½ lemon
salt and ground black pepper

**1** To make the stuffing, put the oil and bacon into a pan and cook over medium heat, stirring occasionally, for 3 minutes without browning. Add the leek and garlic and cook for 3–5 minutes, stirring occasionally, until soft and beginning to brown. Remove from the heat. Stir in the laverbread, breadcrumbs, lemon rind and juice, and seasoning. Leave to cool. Preheat the oven to 200°C/400°F/Gas 6.

**2** Rinse the chicken inside and out, and pat dry with kitchen paper. Spoon the stuffing into the neck cavity and fold the skin over and under. Excess stuffing can be put under the breast skin – loosen it carefully by sliding your fingers underneath and then fill the resulting pocket evenly.

**3** Put the onion, lemon and garlic into the cavity of the chicken. Sit it in a roasting pan and brush with olive oil or melted butter. Cover the breast with foil.

**4** Put into the hot oven and cook for 1½ hours, until the chicken is cooked through (the juices should run clear). Remove the foil for the final 30 minutes of cooking. Remove from the oven and leave to rest in a warm place for 15–20 minutes before carving. Reheat the pan juices and serve spooned over the chicken.

Per portion Energy 486kcal/2027kJ; Protein 33.4g; Carbohydrate 22.3g, of which sugars 1.2g; Fat 29.7g, of which saturates 8.1g; Cholesterol 154mg; Calcium 54mg; Fibre 1g; Sodium 461mg

# duck with damson and ginger

The 19th-century recipe from which this dish has evolved involved salting a whole bird for three days before cooking. Slices of the duck were often served with sharp-tasting fruit sauce. Pan-fried duck breasts go well with a fruit sauce too, as in this recipe.

**3** Score the fat on the duck breast. Do not cut the meat. Brush oil over both sides of the duck. Season the fat side.

**4** Preheat a griddle or frying pan. Cook the duck, skin side down, over medium heat for 5 minutes, until the fat is crisp. Turn over and cook for 4–5 minutes. Leave to rest for 5–10 minutes. Slice diagonally and serve with the sauce.

**Serves 4**

250g/9oz fresh damsons
5ml/1 tsp ground ginger
45ml/3 tbsp water, plus
   a little extra if needed
45ml/3 tbsp sugar
10ml/2 tsp wine vinegar
   or sherry vinegar
4 duck breast portions
15ml/1 tbsp oil
salt and ground black pepper

**1** Put the damsons in a pan with the ginger and water. Bring to the boil, cover and simmer gently for 5 minutes, or until the fruit is soft. Stir frequently and add a little water if it is drying out or sticking to the pan.

**2** Stir in the sugar and vinegar. Press the mixture through a sieve (strainer) to remove stones (pits) and skin. Add more sugar if needed. Season to taste.

Per portion Energy 275kcal/1157kJ; Protein 29.9g; Carbohydrate 17.5g, of which sugars 17.5g; Fat 12.5g, of which saturates 2.4g; Cholesterol 165mg; Calcium 39mg; Fibre 1.1g; Sodium 167mg

# oven-cooked potatoes with bacon

This Carmarthenshire dish, *Tatw rhost a bacwn*, is often called Miser's Feast.
Originally, the potatoes, onions and slices of bacon would have been layered
in the cooking pot with water and then cooked over an open fire.

**Serves 4**

8 thick rindless bacon rashers (strips)
15ml/1 tbsp oil
25g/1oz/2 tbsp butter
2 onions, thinly sliced
1kg/2¼lb potatoes, thinly sliced
600ml/1 pint/2½ cups chicken or
    vegetable stock (or a mixture)
ground black pepper
chopped fresh parsley, to garnish

**1** Preheat the oven to 190°C/375°F/
Gas 5. Chop the bacon. Heat the oil
and butter in a wide flameproof
casserole, add the bacon and cook
over medium heat, stirring occasionally,
until the bacon is beginning to brown.

**2** Add the sliced onions. Cook for
5–10 minutes, stirring, until they have
softened slightly and turned golden.

**3** Add the potatoes. Stir well. Add the
stock, pushing the potatoes down into
the liquid. Season with black pepper.
Bring to the boil, cover and put in the
oven. Cook for 30–40 minutes.

**4** Remove the lid. Raise the heat to
220°C/425°F/Gas 7 and cook for
15–20 minutes more, until the top is
crisp and golden. Garnish with parsley.

Per portion Energy 385kcal/1615kJ; Protein 14.8g; Carbohydrate 48.2g, of which sugars 8.9g; Fat 16.1g, of which saturates 7.1g; Cholesterol 43mg; Calcium 44mg; Fibre 3.9g; Sodium 935mg

# bacon with parsley sauce

This recipe, *Bacwn gyda saws persli*, used to require soaking salty bacon in several changes of cold water before cooking. Today, bacon is less salty and can be brought to the boil in cold water and then drained, achieving a classic taste in much less time.

### Serves 6–8

piece of bacon, such as corner or
   collar, weighing about 1.3kg/3lb
1 large onion, thickly sliced
1 large carrot, thickly sliced
2 celery sticks, roughly chopped
6 black peppercorns
4 whole cloves
2 bay leaves
handful of fresh parsley
600ml/1 pint/2½ cups milk
25g/1oz/2 tbsp butter
25g/1oz/¼ cup plain
   (all-purpose) flour
salt and ground black pepper

### Cook's tip

Use the bacon stock to make a cawl (broth) with vegetables and lentils.

**1** Put the bacon in a large pan and cover it with cold water. Bring the water slowly to the boil, then drain off and discard it. If necessary, rinse the pan and replace the bacon.

**2** Add the onion, carrot, celery, peppercorns, cloves and bay leaves to the bacon in the pan. Pour in enough cold water to cover the bacon by about 2.5cm/1in or slightly more.

**3** Bring slowly to the boil and, if necessary, skim any scum off the surface. Cover and simmer very gently for 1 hour 20 minutes.

**4** To make the parsley sauce, finely chop the parsley and set aside. Put the milk, butter and flour into a pan. Stirring continuously with a whisk, cook over medium heat until the sauce thickens and comes to the boil. Stir in the parsley and let the sauce bubble gently for 1–2 minutes before seasoning to taste with salt and pepper.

**5** Lift the bacon on to a warmed serving plate, cover with foil and leave to rest for 15 minutes before slicing and serving with the parsley sauce.

Per portion Energy 467kcal/1937kJ; Protein 32.7g; Carbohydrate 5.7g, of which sugars 3.7g; Fat 34.8g, of which saturates 14.4g; Cholesterol 87mg; Calcium 118mg; Fibre 0.4g; Sodium 2045mg

# lamb broth

Traditionally, *Cawl Mamgu* or 'granny's broth' would have been made with bony pieces of lamb and beef, usually from the neck or shin – full of flavour and cheap. A large pot of cawl may well have fed a family for several days, with extra ingredients added each time it was reheated – many said that the best cawl was the very last bowlful.

**Serves 4**

30ml/2 tbsp olive oil
2 onions, roughly chopped
2 celery sticks, thickly sliced
2 carrots, thickly sliced
2 parsnips, roughly chopped
1 small swede (rutabaga),
   roughly chopped
800g/1¾lb lamb, such as boned
   shoulder, trimmed and cut into
   bitesize pieces
lamb or vegetable stock
30ml/2 tbsp chopped fresh thyme
   leaves or 10ml/2 tsp dried thyme
3 potatoes
2 leeks, trimmed
handful of chopped fresh parsley
salt and ground black pepper

**1** Heat a large pan, add half the oil and stir in the onions, celery, carrots, parsnips and swede. Cook, stirring occasionally, until golden brown and then lift out.

**2** Add the remaining oil to the pan, quickly brown the lamb in batches and lift out.

**3** Return the browned lamb and vegetables to the pan and pour over enough stock to cover the ingredients. Add the thyme and a little seasoning. Bring to the boil and skim off any surface scum. Cover and cook gently, so that the liquid barely bubbles, for about 1½ hours, until the lamb is tender.

**4** Peel and cut the potatoes into cubes and add to the pan. Cover and cook gently for 15–20 minutes until just soft.

**5** Thinly slice the white part of the leeks and add to the pan, adjust the seasoning to taste and cook for 5 minutes.

**6** Before serving, thinly slice the green parts of the leeks and add to the broth with the parsley. Cook for a few minutes until the leeks soften, and serve.

Per portion Energy 594kcal/2488kJ; Protein 45.2g; Carbohydrate 39.4g, of which sugars 17.9g; Fat 29.6g, of which saturates 11.5g; Cholesterol 152mg; Calcium 151mg; Fibre 8.5g; Sodium 224mg

# minted lamb with leeks and honey

Mint, together with thyme and savory, has always been a significant culinary herb in Wales and mint's particular affinity with lamb is indisputable. In Welsh, this dish is known as *Cig oen â mintys gyda chennin a mêl*. The lamb is marinated in a mixture of oil, lemon juice and fresh mint before it is pan-fried.

### Serves 2

30ml/2 tbsp olive oil
15ml/1 tbsp fresh lemon juice
30ml/2 tbsp finely chopped
   fresh mint leaves
4 lamb chops or steaks
250g/9oz/2 cups leeks, thinly sliced
1 garlic clove, finely chopped
   or crushed
45ml/3 tbsp double (heavy) cream
10ml/2 tsp clear honey
salt and ground black pepper

### Variation

This recipe also works well with rosemary instead of mint. Strip the tender young leaves from a small sprig and chop them finely.

**1** In a shallow, non-metal container, mix 15ml/1 tbsp of the olive oil with the lemon juice, a little seasoning and 15ml/1 tbsp of the chopped fresh mint. Add the lamb and turn until well coated with the mint mixture. If time allows, cover and leave to stand for 30 minutes (or longer in the refrigerator), turning the lamb over occasionally.

**2** Heat a frying pan and add the remaining oil and the lamb. Cook over medium heat for 6–8 minutes each side or until browned and cooked to your liking. Lift out and keep warm.

**3** Pour about 15ml/1 tbsp of fat from the frying pan into a clean pan. Add the leeks and garlic.

**4** Cover and cook over medium heat for about 5 minutes, stirring occasionally, until the leeks are soft.

**5** Stir in the remaining mint with the cream and honey, and heat gently until bubbling. Adjust the seasoning. Serve the leek sauce with the lamb.

Per portion Energy 521kcal/2166kJ; Protein 31.8g; Carbohydrate 7.9g, of which sugars 7g; Fat 40.5g, of which saturates 17g; Cholesterol 145mg; Calcium 54mg; Fibre 2.8g; Sodium 137mg

# loin of saltmarsh lamb with laverbread sauce

Laverbread goes particularly well with saltmarsh lamb. It makes a delicious sauce with milk that has been infused with vegetables and spices.

**Serves 6**

100g/3¾oz dry bread
50g/2oz/½ cup fine or medium oatmeal
1 small onion, roughly chopped
5ml/1 tsp fresh rosemary leaves
grated rind of ½ orange
boned loin of saltmarsh lamb,
    weighing about 1kg/2¼lb
1 small onion, roughly chopped
1 small carrot, roughly chopped
1 small celery stick, roughly chopped
a few black peppercorns
a few allspice berries (optional)
1 bay leaf
450ml/¾ pint/scant 2 cups milk
30ml/2 tbsp plain (all-purpose) flour
30ml/2 tbsp laverbread
salt and ground black pepper

**1** Preheat the oven to 200°C/400°F/Gas 6. Process the bread, oatmeal, onion, rosemary, orange rind and seasoning in a food processor until finely chopped and sticking together. Alternatively, grate the bread, chop the onion and mix by hand.

**2** Open up the lamb and place on a board, skin side down. Spread the stuffing in a thick sausage down the centre. Roll the lamb back up to enclose the stuffing. Secure with string in several places. Place in a roasting pan. Put in the hot oven and cook for 15 minutes, then reduce the temperature to 160°C/325°F/Gas 3. Cook for 30–40 minutes, until the lamb is cooked to your liking.

**3** Meanwhile, put the onion, carrot, celery, peppercorns, allspice (if using) and bay leaf in a pan and add the milk. Heat slowly and, as soon as the milk boils, remove from the heat. Leave to stand for at least 15 minutes to allow the flavours to infuse.

**4** Allow the lamb to rest for 15 minutes. Pour any excess fat from the pan, leaving 15–30ml/1–2 tbsp. Strain the milk into the pan and stir in the flour with a whisk. Cook over medium heat, stirring, until it thickens and comes to the boil. Stir in the laverbread and bubble gently for 1–2 minutes. Season and serve with the lamb.

Per portion Energy 406kcal/1704kJ; Protein 36.4g; Carbohydrate 21.6g, of which sugars 2.9g; Fat 20g, of which saturates 8.8g; Cholesterol 127mg; Calcium 77mg; Fibre 2.1g; Sodium 256mg

# katt pie

These delicious sweet-savoury *Pastai Katt* were traditionally made for the annual fair at Templeton in Pembrokeshire. The lamb, sugar and currants would have been layered inside pies made with suet pastry. This recipe uses a crisp shortcrust pastry made with equal quantities of lard and butter. Serve with a salad of watercress, baby spinach leaves and red onion.

### Serves 6

300g/11oz lean minced (ground) lamb, such as shoulder
75g/3oz/⅓ cup currants
75g/3oz/6 tbsp dark muscovado (molasses) sugar
salt and ground black pepper
milk, for brushing

### For the pastry

250g/9oz/2¼ cups plain (all-purpose) flour
75g/3oz/6 tbsp chilled lard, cut into small cubes
75g/3oz/6 tbsp chilled butter, cut into small cubes
60–75ml/4–5 tbsp cold water

**1** To make the pastry, sift the flour and a pinch of salt into a bowl. Add the lard and butter. With the fingertips, rub the fat into the flour until the mixture resembles fine breadcrumbs. Alternatively, you can process the mixture in a food processor. Stir in the cold water until the mixture can be gathered together into a smooth dough. Wrap it and chill for 20–30 minutes.

**2** Preheat the oven to 190°C/375°F/Gas 5. Mix together the lamb, currants and sugar with a little salt and pepper.

**3** On a lightly floured surface, roll out two-thirds of the dough into a circle. Use it to line a 20–23cm/8–9in tart tin (pan). Spread the lamb mixture over the pastry. Roll out the remaining pastry to make a lid and lay this on top of the lamb filling, then trim off the excess pastry and pinch the edges together to seal them. Make a small slit in the centre of the pastry and brush the top with milk.

**4** Put the pie in the oven and cook for 40 minutes, until the pastry is crisp and golden brown and the filling is cooked. Serve warm or at room temperature.

Per portion Energy 527kcal/2206kJ; Protein 13.9g; Carbohydrate 54g, of which sugars 22.2g; Fat 29.9g, of which saturates 14.7g; Cholesterol 77mg; Calcium 88mg; Fibre 1.5g; Sodium 114mg

# braised beef with vegetables

Stews such as *Cig eidion brwysiedig gyda llysiau* were the mainstay of the Welsh kitchen, when everything was left to cook all day long in one large pot on the range or (in earlier times) on the edge of the fire. Gentle simmering in a modern oven produces an equally delicious dish. 'Trollies', a form of dumpling made with oatmeal and currants, can be added to replace the potatoes.

### Serves 4–6

1kg/2¼lb lean stewing steak,
    cut into 5cm/2in cubes
45ml/3 tbsp plain (all-purpose)
    flour, seasoned
45ml/3 tbsp oil
1 large onion, thinly sliced
1 large carrot, thickly sliced
2 celery sticks, finely chopped
300ml/½ pint/1¼ cups beef stock
30ml/2 tbsp tomato purée (paste)
5ml/1 tsp dried mixed herbs
15ml/1 tbsp dark muscovado
    (molasses) sugar
225g/8oz baby potatoes, halved
2 leeks, thinly sliced
salt and ground black pepper

**1** Preheat the oven to 150°C/300°F/Gas 2. Coat the beef in the seasoned flour. Heat the oil in a large, flameproof casserole. Cook the beef, in small batches, quickly until browned on all sides. With a slotted spoon, lift out and set aside.

**2** Add the vegetables to the casserole and cook over medium heat for 10 minutes, stirring, until they begin to soften and brown. Return the meat to the casserole and add the stock, tomato purée, herbs and sugar, scraping up any sediment that has stuck to the casserole. Heat until the liquid nearly comes to the boil.

**3** Cover with a tight fitting lid and put in the oven. Cook for 2–2½ hours, until the beef is tender. Add the potatoes and leeks, cover and cook for 30 minutes more.

### Variation

To make trollies, sift 175g/6oz/1½ cups self-raising (self-rising) flour and stir in 75g/3oz/½ cup shredded suet (US chilled, grated shortening) and 30ml/2 tbsp chopped parsley. Season. Add water to make a dough, divide into 12 balls, add with the leeks and cook for 15–20 minutes.

Per portion Energy 450kcal/1880kJ; Protein 41.3g; Carbohydrate 23.6g, of which sugars 10.3g; Fat 21.7g, of which saturates 7.3g; Cholesterol 97mg; Calcium 63mg; Fibre 3.5g; Sodium 137mg

# faggots with onion gravy

In the days when most households reared a pig at the bottom of the garden, these *Ffagod* were made with the fresh liver on slaughter day. Serve the faggots with peas.

## Serves 4

450g/1lb pig's liver, trimmed
300g/11oz belly pork
2 onions, roughly chopped
100g/3¾oz/1 cup fresh breadcrumbs
1 egg, beaten
2 sage leaves, chopped
2.5ml/½ tsp ground mace
150ml/¼ pint/⅔ cup beef or
   vegetable stock
butter, for greasing
salt and ground black pepper

### For the onion gravy

50g/2oz/¼ cup butter
4 onions (white or red), thinly sliced
generous 10ml/2 tsp sugar
15ml/1 tbsp plain (all-purpose) flour
300ml/½ pint/1¼ cups beef stock
300ml/½ pint/1¼ cups vegetable stock

**1** Preheat the oven to 180°C/350°F/Gas 4. Roughly chop the liver and pork and place in a food processor with the onions. Process until finely chopped. Then turn the mixture out into a large mixing bowl and stir in the breadcrumbs, egg, sage, 5ml/1 tsp salt, mace and 1.5ml/¼ tsp pepper until thoroughly combined.

**2** With wet hands, shape the mixture into 10–12 round faggots and lay them in a shallow ovenproof dish. Pour in the stock. Use a buttered sheet of foil to cover the dish, butter side down. Crimp the edges around the dish to seal them.

**3** Cook the faggots in the oven for 45–50 minutes, until the juices run clear when pierced with a sharp knife.

**4** For the gravy, melt the butter in a pan. Add the onions and sugar. Cover and cook gently for 30 minutes, until the onions are soft and a rich golden brown. Stir in the flour, remove from the heat and stir in both stocks. Return to the heat and, stirring, bring to the boil. Simmer gently for 20–30 minutes, stirring occasionally (if the liquid is reducing too much, add a splash of water). Season to taste.

**5** Once cooked, remove the foil from the faggots and increase the temperature to 200°C/400°F/Gas 6. Cook for 10 minutes more, then serve with the onion gravy.

Per portion Energy 664kcal/2768kJ; Protein 41.4g; Carbohydrate 31.2g, of which sugars 9.8g; Fat 42.5g, of which saturates 17.9g; Cholesterol 421mg; Calcium 84mg; Fibre 2.2g; Sodium 434mg

# puddings

The Welsh will readily extol the virtues of simple, traditional puddings made with milk, bread or fruit, such as the classic Monmouth pudding. Another much-loved Welsh pudding is fruit pie, made with apples, plums, damsons, gooseberries, rhubarb, or the favourite of the region, whinberries. Before ovens were invented, puddings were cooked on a flat bakestone over the fire.

*Left: Crisp orchard fruits and freshly picked wild berries are combined with luxuriant cream to create irresistible hot and cold desserts.*

# Snowdon pudding

This light pudding was allegedly created for a hotel at the base of Wales' highest peak.
Use the softest, juiciest raisins you can find – they are more likely to stick to the basin.

### Serves 6

15–25g/½–1oz/1–2 tbsp butter
100g/3¾oz/⅔ cup raisins
finely grated rind of 1 lemon
175g/6oz/3 cups fresh
   white breadcrumbs
75g/3oz/½ cup shredded suet
   (US chilled, grated shortening)
75g/3oz/6 tbsp soft brown sugar
25g/1oz/¼ cup cornflour (cornstarch)
2 eggs
60ml/4 tbsp orange marmalade
30ml/2 tbsp fresh lemon juice

### For the sauce

1 lemon
25g/1oz/¼ cup cornflour (cornstarch)
300ml/½ pint/1¼ cups milk
50g/2oz/¼ cup caster (superfine) sugar
25g/1oz/2 tbsp butter

**1** Soften the butter and then smear it on the inside of a 1.2-litre/2-pint pudding bowl. Press half the raisins on the buttered surface.

**2** Reserve a pinch of lemon rind and mix the rest with the breadcrumbs, suet, brown sugar, cornflour and the remaining raisins. Beat the eggs with the marmalade and lemon juice and stir into the dry ingredients.

**3** Spoon the mixture into the bowl, without disturbing the raisins. Cover with baking parchment (pleated) and then a large sheet of foil (also pleated). Tuck the edges under and press tightly to the sides. Steam over a pan of boiling water for 1¾ hours.

**4** Meanwhile, make the sauce. Pare two or three large strips of lemon rind and put into a pan with 150ml/¼ pint/⅔ cup water. Bring to the boil and simmer for 10 minutes. Discard the rind. Blend the cornflour with the milk and stir into the pan. Squeeze the juice from half the lemon and add to the pan with the sugar and butter. Heat until the sauce thickens and comes to the boil.

**5** Turn the pudding out on to a warmed plate, spoon the sauce over the top and sprinkle with the reserved lemon rind.

Per portion Energy 456kcal/1922kJ; Protein 7.7g; Carbohydrate 74.4g, of which sugars 43.4g; Fat 16.8g, of which saturates 8.6g; Cholesterol 82mg; Calcium 131mg; Fibre 1.1g; Sodium 304mg

# whinberry and apple tart

The wild harvest of whinberries (elsewhere called bilberries, blueberries or whortleberries) was traditionally gathered with great excitement from the hillsides in summer and most often made into tarts, such as this *Tarten lus ac afalau*.

**Serves 6**

2 cooking apples, total
    weight about 400g/14oz,
    peeled and cored
10ml/2 tsp cornflour (cornstarch)
350g/12oz/3 cups whinberries
40–50g/3–4 tbsp caster (superfine)
    sugar, plus extra for sprinkling
milk, for brushing

**For the pastry**

250g/9oz/2¼ cups plain
    (all-purpose) flour
25g/1oz/2 tbsp caster
    (superfine) sugar
150g/5oz/10 tbsp butter,
    chilled and cut into
    small cubes
1 egg

**1** To make the pastry, sift the flour into a bowl and stir in the sugar. Add the butter and rub into the flour until it resembles fine crumbs. Stir in the egg and enough cold water to form a smooth dough. Wrap it and chill for 20–30 minutes.

**2** Preheat the oven to 190°C/375°F/Gas 5. On a lightly floured surface, roll out half the dough to make a circle and use it to line a deep 23cm/9in tart tin (pan) or ovenproof dish, pressing it into the corners and allowing it to hang over the sides. Roll out the remaining pastry to form a circle large enough for a lid.

**3** Chop the apples into small pieces and toss with the cornflour until evenly coated. Arrange them in the bottom of the pastry case, scatter the whinberries on top and sprinkle the sugar over. Lightly brush the edges of the pastry with water.

**4** Lay the pastry lid over the fruit filling. Trim off the excess pastry and pinch the edges together to seal them well. Make a small slit in the centre, then brush the top with milk and sprinkle with a little sugar.

**5** Put in the oven and cook for 30–40 minutes until the pastry is crisp and golden and the filling is cooked. While the pastry is still hot, sprinkle with caster sugar.

Per portion Energy 403kcal/1688kJ; Protein 5.76g; Carbohydrate 51.4g, of which sugars 18.15g; Fat 20.8g, of which saturates 12.5g; Cholesterol 81.5mg; Calcium 98.6mg; Fibre 3.5g; Sodium 157.5mg

# Monmouth pudding

Similar to the English Queen of Puddings, in *Pwdin Mynwy* red jam is layered with milk-drenched breadcrumbs, set with eggs. In the English version, the egg whites are whisked into meringue and cooked on top of the breadcrumb and jam layers.

### Serves 4

450ml/¾ pint/scant 2 cups milk
25g/1oz/2 tbsp caster
  (superfine) sugar
finely grated rind of 1 lemon
175g/6oz/3 cups fresh
  white breadcrumbs
2 eggs, separated
60ml/4 tbsp strawberry,
  raspberry or other red jam

**1** Put the milk, sugar and rind into a pan and bring to the boil. Pour over the breadcrumbs and leave for 15 minutes.

**2** Preheat the oven to 150°C/300°F/ Gas 2 and butter a 23cm/9in ovenproof dish. Stir the egg yolks into the breadcrumb mixture. Whisk the whites until stiff peaks form and fold them into the breadcrumb mixture.

**3** Melt the jam and drizzle half of it into the bottom of the prepared dish.

**4** Spoon half the breadcrumb mixture on top, gently levelling the surface, and drizzle the rest of the jam over it. Spread the remaining breadcrumb mixture over the pudding. Put in the oven and cook for 30–40 minutes, until golden brown. Serve warm.

Per portion Energy 309kcal/1313kJ; Protein 12g; Carbohydrate 57.1g, of which sugars 24.3g; Fat 5.4g, of which saturates 1.9g; Cholesterol 101mg; Calcium 205mg; Fibre 1g; Sodium 418mg

# chilled fruit pudding

This trifle-like dish, *Pwdin frwythau oeredig*, uses thick natural yogurt to give a lighter touch than an all-cream topping. The Welsh have always used flowers in their cooking and the elderflower cordial adds its fragrance to the topping.

**Serves 4–6**

550g/1lb 4oz mixed soft fruit
50g/2oz/4 tbsp sugar
large thick slice of bread with crusts removed, about 125g/4½oz
300ml/½ pint/1¼ cups double (heavy) cream
45ml/3 tbsp elderflower cordial
150ml/¼ pint/⅔ cup thick natural (plain) yogurt

**1** Reserve a few of the soft fruits for decoration, then put the remainder into a pan with the sugar and 30ml/2 tbsp water. Bring just to the boil, cover and simmer gently for 4–5 minutes until the fruit is soft and lots of juice has formed.

**2** Cut the bread into cubes, measuring about 2.5cm/1in, and put them into a large dish or individual serving bowls.

**3** Spoon the fruit over and cool.

**4** Whip the cream with the cordial until stiff peaks begin to form. Gently stir in the yogurt and spoon the mixture over the top of the fruit.

**5** Chill until required. Just before serving, decorate the top with the reserved fruit.

**Cook's tip**
A bag of mixed frozen fruit is ideal for this dessert.

Per portion Energy 382kcal/1592kJ; Protein 5.2g; Carbohydrate 29.9g, of which sugars 20.2g; Fat 27.8g, of which saturates 16.9g; Cholesterol 69mg; Calcium 124mg; Fibre 2.6g; Sodium 144mg

# bread pudding

Welsh cooks, just like those in other parts of Britain, were extremely inventive with the stale ends of loaves. Serve this spicy, rich and filling dish warm with custard or cream.

### Serves 9

225g/8oz stale bread, weighed after
    removing crusts
300ml/½ pint/1¼ cups milk
butter, for greasing
50g/1¾oz/4 tbsp dark muscovado
    (molasses) sugar
85g/3oz/⅓ cup shredded suet
    (US chilled, grated shortening)
    or grated chilled butter
225g/8oz/1⅓ cups mixed dried fruit,
    including currants, sultanas (golden
    raisins), finely chopped citrus peel
15ml/1 tbsp mixed (apple pie) spice
2.5ml/½ tsp freshly grated nutmeg
finely grated rind of 1 small orange
    and 1 small lemon, plus a little
    orange or lemon juice
1 egg, lightly beaten
caster (superfine) sugar, for sprinkling

**1** Break the bread into small pieces. Place in a large mixing bowl, pour the milk over and leave for about 30 minutes.

**2** Preheat the oven to 180°C/350°F/Gas 4. Butter an 18cm/7in square and 5cm/2in deep ovenproof dish.

**3** Using a fork, break up the bread before stirring in the sugar, suet, dried fruit, spices and citrus rinds. Beat in the egg, adding some orange or lemon juice to make a soft mixture.

**4** Spread the mixture into the prepared dish and level the surface. Put in the hot oven and cook for about 1¼ hours or until the top is brown and firm to the touch.

**5** Sprinkle caster sugar over the surface and allow to cool before cutting it into nine squares.

### Cook's tip

Although suet is traditional in this pudding, you could use grated chilled butter, if you prefer.

Per portion Energy 254kcal/1072kJ; Protein 4.3g; Carbohydrate 39.7g, of which sugars 27g; Fat 10.2g, of which saturates 5.3g; Cholesterol 31mg; Calcium 103mg; Fibre 1.4g; Sodium 147mg

# breads
# and cakes

Baking day and tea-time have long been traditions in Wales, with mountains of bread and spiced cakes to take the family through the week. Nowhere has the bakestone been more utilized than in the Welsh kitchen, to make griddle cakes and bread.

There are cakes that can be rustled up for unexpected guests and cakes that will keep for several days, ready to fill out the lunch boxes of hard-working hill farmers, miners, quarry workers and fishermen.

*Left: The classic Bara Brith tea bread is just one of the many culinary delights to be savoured from the Welsh kitchen.*

# bakestone bread

A loaf of bread that is cooked on the hob – watch it rise and marvel! The finished
*Bara planc* has a distinctive appearance with a soft texture and scorched crust.

## Makes 1 loaf

500g/1lb 2oz/4¼ cups plain
   (all-purpose) flour
5ml/1 tsp fine sea salt
5ml/1 tsp sugar
7.5ml/1½ tsp easy-blend
   (rapid-rise) dried yeast
150ml/¼ pint/⅔ cup milk
15g/½oz/1 tbsp butter,
   cut into small pieces
5ml/1 tsp oil

## Cooks tips

• If you have a bread machine,
you can use it in this recipe. Use
it on a short programme to make
the dough and then continue with
steps 3–5.
• Make sure to use ordinary plain
flour and not strong bread flour.

**1** Put the flour into a large bowl and add the salt, sugar and yeast. Combine the
milk with 150ml/¼ pint/⅔ cup water and add the butter. Heat gently until lukewarm.
Stir the liquid into the flour, then gather it together to make a dough ball.

**2** Tip the dough on to a lightly floured surface and knead until smooth, firm and
elastic. Then put the oil in a large bowl and turn the dough in it until it is lightly
coated. Cover the dough with clear film (plastic wrap) or a damp dish towel
and leave to rise for about 1½ hours, or until just about doubled in size.

**3** Tip the dough out on to a lightly floured surface and knead gently, just until it
becomes smooth, soft and stretchy. On the same floured surface and using your
hands or a rolling pin, press the dough into a rough circle measuring about 20cm/
8in in diameter and 2cm/¾in thick. Leave to stand for 15 minutes.

**4** Meanwhile, heat a bakestone or heavy frying pan over a medium heat. Lift the
dough on to the warm surface and cook gently for 20 minutes.

**5** Turn the bread over – it may sink, but will soon start rising again. Gently
cook the second side for about 20 minutes. The top and bottom crusts should
be firm and browned, while the sides remain pale. Leave to cool on a wire rack.

Per loaf Energy 1928kcal/8179kJ; Protein 52.2g; Carbohydrate 399.8g, of which sugars 18.8g; Fat 24.4g, of which saturates 10.8g; Cholesterol 41mg; Calcium 885mg; Fibre 15.5g; Sodium 2136mg

# bara brith teabread

This spiced loaf has become widely known as Bara Brith, though the method of making it is nothing like the original yeasted bread. Once the fruit has been plumped up by soaking it in tea, this version is quick to make with self-raising flour. You can toast and butter it, but it also tastes just as good as it is.

**Makes 1 large loaf**

225g/8oz/1⅓ cups mixed
   dried fruit and chopped
   mixed (candied) peel
225ml/8fl oz/1 cup hot strong
   tea, strained
225g/8oz/2 cups self-raising
   (self rising) flour
5ml/1 tsp mixed (apple pie) spice
25g/1oz/2 tbsp butter
100g/3¾oz/8 tbsp soft
   brown sugar
1 egg, lightly beaten

**Cook's tip**

The flavour of the loaf can be varied subtly by using a different tea – try the distinctive perfume of Earl Grey.

**1** Put the fruit in a heatproof bowl and pour over the hot tea. Cover and leave to stand at room temperature for several hours or overnight.

**2** Preheat the oven to 180°C/350°F/Gas 4. Grease a 900g/2lb loaf tin (pan) and line it with baking parchment.

**3** Sift the flour and the mixed spice into a large mixing bowl. Add the butter and, with your fingertips, rub it into the flour until the mixture starts to resemble fine breadcrumbs.

**4** Stir in the sugar, then add the fruit and its liquid along with the beaten egg. Stir well to make a mixture with a soft consistency.

**5** Transfer the mixture to the prepared loaf tin and level the surface.

**6** Put in the preheated oven and cook for about 1 hour or until a skewer inserted into the centre comes out clean. Turn out on to a wire rack and leave to cool completely.

Per loaf Energy 2024kcal/8588kJ; Protein 33.2g; Carbohydrate 432.7g, of which sugars 261.3g; Fat 29.9g, of which saturates 15g; Cholesterol 244mg; Calcium 565mg; Fibre 11.9g; Sodium 342mg

# old-fashioned treacle cake

Like other quick-to-make cakes, *Teisen driog hen ffasiwn* would have been baked on an enamel plate. The treacle gives it a rich colour and a deep flavour, and the sight of it must have been most welcome to miners and other workers when they opened their 'box' during their well-earned meal break.

### Makes a 20cm/8in cake

butter, for greasing
250g/9oz/2 cups self-raising
   (self-rising) flour
2.5ml/½ tsp mixed (apple pie) spice
75g/3oz/6 tbsp butter,
   cut into small cubes
25g/1oz/2 tbsp caster
   (superfine) sugar
150g/5oz/1 cup mixed dried fruit
1 egg
15ml/1 tbsp black treacle (molasses)
100ml/3½fl oz/scant ½ cup milk

### Cook's tip

Vary the fruit – try using chopped ready-to-eat dried apricots and stem ginger, or a packet of luxury dried fruit.

**1** Preheat the oven to 180°C/350°F/Gas 4. Butter a shallow 20–23cm/8–9in ovenproof flan dish or baking tin (pan).

**2** Sift the flour and spice into a large mixing bowl. Add the butter and, with your fingertips, rub it into the flour until the mixture resembles fine crumbs. Alternatively, you could do this in a food processor. Stir in the sugar and mixed dried fruit.

**3** Beat the egg and, with a small whisk or a fork, stir in the treacle and then the milk. Stir the liquid into the flour to make a fairly stiff but moist consistency, adding a little extra milk if necessary. Transfer the cake mixture to the prepared dish or tin with a spoon and level out the surface.

**4** Bake the cake in the hot oven for about 1 hour until it has risen, is firm to the touch and fully cooked through. To check if the cake is cooked, insert a small skewer into the centre – it should come out free of sticky mixture.

**5** Leave the cooked treacle cake to cool completely. Serve cut into rough wedges, straight from the dish.

Per cake Energy 2089kcal/8805kJ; Protein 37.4g; Carbohydrate 343g, of which sugars 152.4g; Fat 72.8g, of which saturates 42.2g; Cholesterol 356mg; Calcium 720mg; Fibre 11.1g; Sodium 676mg

# Welsh cakes

These speckled discs were traditionally cooked at least once a week in kitchens throughout Wales. Their Welsh name, *Pice ar y maen*, means 'cakes on the stone'.

**Makes about 16**

250g/9oz/2 cups plain (all-purpose) flour
7.5ml/1½ tsp baking powder
125g/4½oz/½ cup butter, cut into small cubes
100g/3½oz/½ cup caster (superfine) sugar, plus extra for dusting
75g/3oz/½ cup currants
1 egg, lightly beaten
45ml/3 tbsp milk

**1** Heat a bakestone or heavy frying pan over medium to low heat.

**2** Sift the flour, baking powder and a pinch of salt into a mixing bowl. Rub in the butter. Stir in the sugar and currants.

**3** With a cutting action and a round-ended knife, stir in the egg with enough milk to gather the dough into a ball.

**4** Transfer to a lightly floured surface and roll out to about 5mm/¼in thick. Cut out 6–7.5cm/2½–3in rounds.

**5** Smear a little butter or oil over the hot bakestone or pan and cook the cakes, in batches, for 4–5 minutes on each side or until they are slightly risen, golden and cooked through. Transfer to a wire rack, dust with caster sugar on both sides and leave to cool.

Per portion Energy 154kcal/649kJ; Protein 2.1g; Carbohydrate 22g, of which sugars 10.1g; Fat 7g, of which saturates 4.2g; Cholesterol 29mg; Calcium 36mg; Fibre 0.6g; Sodium 54mg

# Anglesey shortbread

These biscuits, *Teisen Berffro*, originated on Anglesey. The shell motif is made by pressing the dough into a queen scallop shell prior to baking.

### Makes 12

100g/3½oz/½ cup butter, softened
50g/2oz/¼ cup caster (superfine)
 sugar, plus extra for sprinkling
150g/5oz/1¼ cups plain
 (all-purpose) flour

### Cook's tip

Shaping the first biscuit may be tricky, but the shell will coat with sugar and the rest will slip out easily.

**1** Preheat the oven to 200°C/400°F/ Gas 6 and line a baking sheet with baking parchment.

**2** Put the butter and sugar into a bowl and beat until light and fluffy. Sift the flour over and stir it in until the mixture can be gathered into a ball of dough.

**3** Work the dough so that the warmth of your hand keeps the dough soft and pliable. Divide and shape it into 12 balls.

**4** Sprinkle the inside of a scallop shell with sugar, gently press a ball of dough into it, spreading it evenly so the shell is filled. Invert on to the paper-lined sheet, pressing it down to flatten the base and to mark it with the impression of the shell. Carefully lift the shell off. Alternatively, make plain biscuits measuring 5cm/2in across.

**5** Cook in the hot oven for 10 minutes until set. Sprinkle with a little sugar and transfer to a wire rack to cool.

Per portion Energy 121kcal/506kJ; Protein 1.2g; Carbohydrate 14.1g, of which sugars 4.6g; Fat 7g, of which saturates 4.4g; Cholesterol 18mg; Calcium 21mg; Fibre 0.4g; Sodium 51mg

# index